Cave Crystals

Kitchen Experiment

By Meg Gaertner

Published by The Child's World®
1980 Lookout Drive • Mankato, MN 56003-1705
800-599-READ • www.childsworld.com

ISBN 9781503825369
LCCN 2017959695

Printed in the United States of America
PA02378

Table of Contents

CHAPTER 1

Inside a Cave

Have you ever been inside a **cave**? A cave is a large hole. It can be under the ground. It can also be in the side of a hill. Caves have many rocks in them. These rocks can form neat shapes. **Stalactites** grow down from the roof of a cave. They are long and pointy. **Stalagmites** grow up from the floor of the cave.

It can take thousands of years to form these shapes. Water makes them. Water on the roof of a cave holds **minerals**.

The water drips down and leaves minerals behind. They pile on top of each other over time.

Caves are dark inside. We need lights to see stalagmites.

These minerals form the stalactites and stalagmites that we see.

But what is a mineral? A mineral is a **solid** found in nature. It is not living. Salt is a mineral. Wood is not a mineral. Wood comes from trees. Trees are living things.

Some minerals are made from only one thing. Gold is a mineral. It is only made from gold. It is also an **element**. Elements are pure substances. They are made of one type of **atom**. Everything is made of atoms.

TIP
Most stalactites are pointy on the bottom. Most stalagmites are round and flat on the top. This is because of how the water drips.

Water carries minerals down the stalactite. This makes the stalactite longer.

We can add salt to foods like french fries, popcorn, and vegetables.

Atoms are very tiny. We can't see them without special machines.

Some minerals are made from many different things. Salt is made of sodium and chlorine. They are both elements.

Minerals are formed in a very ordered way. The groups of atoms in a mineral form neat rows. It is easy for minerals to grow. New atoms add to the rows that are already there. This is what happens to form stalactites and stalagmites.

CHAPTER 2

Growing Crystals

We can make our own stalagmites and stalactites. We will make them out of **crystals**. Crystals are made of atoms that are neat and ordered. They have many flat sides.

We see crystals all the time. Sugar, salt, and snow are crystals. Look at these things very closely. You will see the flat sides.

TIP

Most minerals are crystals. But not all crystals are minerals. Sugar is a crystal but not a mineral. Sugar comes from a plant, which is a living thing.

Sugar crystals can be pressed together to make sugar cubes.

When you mix salt in water, the salt **dissolves**. It seems to go away. But it is still there. You cannot see the salt, but you can still taste it.

Lemonade is made from lemons, water, and sugar. The sugar dissolves in the water.

The water can only hold so much salt. If you add enough salt, the salt will not dissolve. This means that the water is **saturated**. It cannot hold any more salt.

We put baking soda in cookie dough. It makes the cookies turn brown in the oven.

You will make stalagmites and stalactites out of baking soda. Baking soda is a crystal. It is used for cooking and cleaning. It dissolves in water. To grow crystals, you need more baking soda than water. The water needs to be saturated. If it is not, the crystals will dissolve into the water.

THE EXPERIMENT
Let's Grow Cave Crystals!

MATERIALS LIST

1 piece of string, 3 feet (1 m) long
2 paper clips
baking dish
2 glasses
bowl
2 cups (473 mL) warm tap water
1/3 cup (43 g) baking soda
spoon
food coloring

TIME TO PREPARE: 10 minutes

TIME TO COMPLETE:
5 days

1. Fold your string in half. Twist the string together.

2. Put a paper clip on each end of the string. This will weigh it down in the glass.

3. Set the baking dish in a warm place. Put a glass on each side of the baking dish.

TIP

Make sure your water is very saturated with baking soda. If crystals are not growing, add more baking soda to your water.

4. With an adult's help, pour warm tap water into the bowl. Mix baking soda into the warm water with the spoon. Keep adding more baking soda until it stops dissolving.

5. Add a few drops of food coloring to the bowl.

6. Dip the entire string into the bowl. Then fill each glass with the mixture.

7. Put one end of the string in one glass. Put the other end in the other glass. There should be a small dip in the string.

TIP
If there isn't a dip, move the glasses closer together. If the dip is too small, the string will dry out. But if the dip is too big, there will be too much dripping. It will make a mess.

8. Observe the crystals growing every day. After a few days, you may need to add more water or baking soda to each glass.

9. Continue observing the crystals. Are there stalactites? Stalagmites? Can you see the flat sides on the crystals?

Glossary

atom (AT-uhm) An atom is a tiny thing that makes up everything we see. An element is made of one type of atom.

cave (KAYV) A cave is a large hole. A cave can be in the ground or in the side of a hill.

crystals (KRISS-tuhls) Crystals are made of atoms that are neat and ordered. Sugar and salt are crystals.

dissolves (di-ZOLVS) Something dissolves when it seems to fade into something else. Sugar dissolves into water.

element (EL-uh-muhnt) An element is something made of only one kind of atom. Gold is an element.

minerals (MIN-ur-uhls) Minerals are solids found in nature. Minerals cannot be from living things.

saturated (SACH-uh-ray-tuhd) Something is saturated when it can no longer dissolve anything. Sugar water is saturated when you can see sugar on the bottom.

solid (SOL-id) A solid is a type of matter. A solid does not change its shape.

stalactites (stuh-LAK-tites) Stalactites are rocks that grow in a cave. Stalactites hang down from the ceiling of a cave.

stalagmites (stuh-LAG-mites) Stalagmites are rocks that grow in a cave. Stalagmites grow up from the bottom of a cave.

To Learn More

In the Library

Dennie, Devin. *My Book of Rocks and Minerals*. New York, NY:
DK Penguin Random House, 2017.

Ringstad, Arnold. *Underground Habitats*. Mankato, MN:
The Child's World, 2014.

Simon, Seymour. *Rocks and Minerals*. New York, NY:
HarperCollins, 2017.

On the Web

Visit our Web site for links about cave crystals:
childsworld.com/links

Note to Parents, Teachers, and Librarians: We routinely verify our Web links to make
sure they are safe and active sites. So encourage your readers to check them out!

Index

About the Author

Meg Gaertner is a children's book author and editor who lives in Minnesota. When not writing, she enjoys dancing and spending time outdoors.

24